The World's Best Computer Jokes

Rex Malik

The World's Best Computer Jokes

Including the Prize Winning Jokes
from The Times-CMG Humour Competition

ANGUS
& ROBERTSON
PUBLISHERS

ANGUS & ROBERTSON PUBLISHERS

Unit 4, Eden Park, 31 Waterloo Road,
North Ryde, NSW, Australia 2113, and
16 Golden Square, London W1R 4BN,
United Kingdom

First published in Australia by
Angus & Robertson Publishers in 1987
First published in the United Kingdom by
Angus & Robertson UK Ltd in 1987

Copyright © Rex Malik 1987

British Library Cataloguing in Publication Data

Malik, Rex
  World's best computer jokes.
  1. Electronic digital computers – Anecdotes,
     facetiae, satire, etc.
  i. Title
  004.0207 QA76.5

ISBN 0-207-15679-4

Typeset in 12pt Palatino by
New Faces, Bedford.

Printed in the United Kingdom by
Hazell Watson & Viney Ltd.

Introduction

This is, quite simply, a book for those who appreciate the significance of the equation:

$$1 + 1 \ \text{☞} = 2$$

where ☞ stands for "very rarely".

This is also the sort of book to give your superiors when they need distraction, and which they might give you when trying to tell you something.

Hopefully, it is the sort of book you buy more than one copy of, because people will tear pages out to share jokes with others by pinning them up on the wall. They do not do this just to increase my royalties, but also because at the first sight of this volume any senior manager with any sense locks up the office copier. Indeed, were it not that this book has in part another sponsor, I would dedicate it to the Xerox Corporation without whose product many of these jokes would not have found such wide currency in the computer community.

Finally, this book is for anyone who curses (as in cursor?), as yet another of those wretched systems, terminals, desk micros, PCs or workstations persists in behaving as it, not the operator, wishes.

It is true that you will not find: 'Why did the computer cross the road?', but many other old favourites are included. Sometimes I have used an early version, sometimes an update: it all depended on what seemed funny at the time.

My thanks are due to the taxpayers and government for supporting NATO which started me off and, over the years, that major contributor Anonymous (often a cover for one of those whom one might expect to know better, and yet without whom most of the ruder, and grosser, jokes would never have been perpetrated).

I am grateful for permissions to quote from *Abacus, Computer,* and *Computer Weekly,* not otherwise attributed in the text.

I am grateful also for the help received from CMG Computer Management Group (UK) Ltd., particularly from Managing Director Ron White. Otherwise, I wish to acknowledge the aid, sometimes unknowing, of Martin Banks, Stan Bootle, Michael Foreman, Barney Gibbens (the world's next best collection of computer jokes), Anthony Gottlieb, Jim Haynes, Matthew May, Ted Nelson, John Pascoe (for cartoon originals from his collection), and Peter White, all of whom either owned or passed on material, or indeed from whom I stole it!

I am also especially grateful to Alan Jenkins of *The Times:* after all the original project which led to this was his fault.

That last bit is another joke. Most of those that follow I think are funnier.

Rex Malik

In the Beginning ...

The following two items seem to have been around since the earliest days of computing.

ACHTUNG!

   Alles Lookenspeepers! Das Komputenmachine ist nicht für gefingerpoken und mittengrabben. Ist easy der Springenwerk schnappen, blowenfusen, und mit Spitzensparken poppenkorken. Ist nicht für bei das Dummkopfen gewerken. Das Rubberneckensightseeren die Hände in das Pockets keepen, relaxen, und watchen das Blinkenlights.

*   *   *

THE PRUDENTIAL ASSURANCE COMPANY LTD
HOLBORN BARS, LONDON, EC1N 2NH

The calculation by computer of policyholders'
bonuses is a new development, and it has been
found that due to a programme specification error
the terminal bonus was understated in the first
print of the certificates. Unfortunately it has
not been possible to prevent the bulk despatch
of these certificates and if you have not already
received the incorrect statement it will be
reaching you shortly.

We apologise for this error and shall be glad if
you will retain the enclosed certificate which
shows the correct figures and <u>destroy</u> the one
previously sent to you.

Two Early Stories
(or Old Soldiers – and Old Soldiers' jokes – never die).

Military HQ: communications were set up, reports were received, intelligence weighed, the situation was evaluated, and data fed into the computer, following all of which the General's staff asked the question: "Do we attack or retreat?"

"Yes," said the computer.

"Yes, what?" said the General crossly.

"Yes, Sir!" said the computer.

*　　　*　　　*

The two US generals are in the control centre buried deep in Cheyenne mountain. One is surveying the outside world through a periscope, through which he can see a nuclear explosion in progress.

The other is looking at a print-out from the defence computers, and worriedly saying:

"Well, that's not what it states here."

*　　　*　　　*

The Times-CMG Computing Humour Competition Winners

Information technology has not escaped the attention of humorists, particularly those immediately concerned with its application. *Ipso facto,* we felt, there must be a huge quantity of computer jokes in general circulation.

In launching The Times/CMG Computing Humour Competition we asked for funny situations which can arise in the office or factory, at the bank, the supermarket checkout or the airline terminal. Every week, for four weeks, we asked *The Times* readers to share with us a joke, a story or a description of a humorous situation involving computers.

We were not disappointed. The following section includes all those which amused, perplexed and confused the judges, and to which they finally, with good humour, conceded victory.

"I was just trying out my new personal financial
planning software package, dear."

Joe Stockton, Great Brickhill, Milton Keynes

"... This one's thin line, thin line, space, thick line, thin line, space, thin line, thick line, space, thin line, thin line ..."

Roger Penwill, New Ash Green, Kent

True Stories

True Story Department: indeed it's a funny old world out there. Among the most entertaining stories submitted were these apparently true slices of life.

But whoever said that reality necessarily had to be original?

Six year old Steven must have been badly behaved that day, for his parents had to collect him from school.

His mother, by profession a computer research analyst (so you can see where he got it from), asked him why.

"Mum," he replied, "when I got up this morning I was programmed to be 'naughty', but it's all right ... I'll be programmed 'good' tomorrow."

R. L. Swink, Richmond, Surrey

*   *   *

Then there was the nine year old who reported:
"We have a new thing at school. It is very small, quick, and very clever.
"It is called a Micro Professor."

Arthur Hawarden, St. Austell, Cornwall

*   *   *

The – carefully unidentified – local government office received and put together its computer system. Then eight local government officers, some of them computer specialists played electrician for hours trying to get it to work. Whatever they did, nothing seemed to happen. Then the office junior came in and turned the screen brightness up.

Mrs J. Bland, Durham

*   *   *

Her job was to check invoices for payment.

She was given a rise for coping with a substantial increase in workload without any need for assistance.

Her comment was that she never wasted time on computer-generated invoices as computers never made mistakes: she just concentrated on the typed ones.

M. J. M. Coverdale, Maidstone, Kent

*   *   *

But they'll try *anything* on you to save themselves from having to work ...

The customer queried the London Electricity Board account and was met with the response that the computer was on a go-slow.

Pauline Asper, London W13

*   *   *

The world's computer industries are trying hard to develop computer translation systems capable of handling almost any language. Here's one of many reasons why:

(Extract from the unpacking instructions that came with a Commodore Printer, Model 1526)

2. Remove shipping screws. Carefully lift front of computer unit and make it stands as bottom of case be vartically face to you and hold the unit by the one of your hand on the soft surface. Then remove the shipping screws with a Phillips-head screw driver. After it is removed, gently back the unit to lay flat on a firm surface, position the printer front be face to you.

Richard G. Hunt, Bromley, Kent

*   *   *

"This accounting software package should suit
you, sir ... It doesn't leave an audit trail."

The Computer Generation

The word processing package on the Apricot PC included a spelling checker, so its new owner proudly set out to test it, intentionally typing ...

'THIS APRICOT IS FULL OF PIPPS!'

On pressing the key for a spelling check, the system replied with its first message:

'This document contains six words.'

Followed by:

'Two words are not in my dictionary.'

Then:

'The first word is: PIPPS.'

So far so good.

Finally ...

'The second word is: APRICOT.'

Malcolm Windsor, Edinburgh

*　　　*　　　*

After heart trouble was suspected, Mr Smith, on a visit to San Francisco, had a check-up at a local computerised diagnostic centre.

The system led the doctor to ask Mr Smith whether he smoked.

"No," he replied.

"Too bad. The indications are cardiac arrest negative, but the computer says stopping smoking would help you."

E. A. D. Smith, Liverpool

*　　　*　　　*

A computer was asked why it was that bread always lands on the floor buttered-side down.

Its answer was that the bread was buttered on the wrong side.

D. L. Shaw, London SW7

*   *   *

The salesman sold a computing system to a far and foreign firm, on visiting which some months later he was alarmed to see it still had covers on.

"Anything wrong?" he asked.

"No," beamed the accounting manager, "throughput has increased, efficiency has improved."

"How's that?"

"Every morning," he said, "I tell the staff, if you don't work harder and more efficiently, that machine is going to replace you."

M. J. M. Coverdale, Maidstone, Kent

*   *   *

Q: What's a split second?
A: It is the amount of time between quitting a program – and realising you have not saved any of the work you have spent the last seven hours on.

Marianne Fry, Norwich

*   *   *

First scientist: "Eureka!" (or whatever they say nowadays). "We have achieved Artificial Intelligence."

Second scientist: "How do you know?" (They are a sceptical lot.)

First scientist: "The computer has just asked for the back of an envelope."

Jim Rhodes, Pulborough, West Sussex

*   *   *

Cartoon by Sam Smith, The Times

The computer consultant was very young when he died and went to Heaven, where he promptly marched up to St. Peter, and demanded:

"Why me?"

"Well," said St. Peter, punching keys on his VDU, "we've had a look at your time sheets.

"According to our records, the amount of time you have been charging clients makes you 82."

John Irving, Norwich

*   *   *

The transatlantic balloonist was lost up in the clouds. Suddenly there was a break. Below was an obvious golf course with just as obvious (if oblivious) a golfer.

"Where am I?" shouted down the balloonist.

"You are in a balloon, 70 feet above the ninth tee of a golf course," replied the startled golfer crossly.

"And you must be a systems analyst," said the balloonist.

The golfer was even more startled.

"I am," he said, "how did you know that?"

"Well," said the balloonist, "the information you gave me was 100 per cent accurate – and totally useless."

E. H. Brooks, Braddan, Isle of Man

*   *   *

She went to a computer dating agency to find the man of her dreams – tall, blond, athletic ...

He arrived – short, fat, and bald.

"I don't think much of your computer," she complained.

"It's not the computer, it's the programmer."

"And what does he look like?" she asked.

"Short, fat and bald."

B. L. Duffen, Redditch, Hereford & Worcester

*   *   *

"One day I'm going to write a user-friendly
program that will still respect me the
next morning."

Tony Reynolds, London N19
Cartoon by Sam Smith, The Times

Groan Groan

The many entries we received ranged from good to bad, but few were indifferent. We said we did not mind old ones recycled, and I know we did not specify how old, but surely there must be a limit, a time bar?

It seems not ...

"When IBM Presidents die, they're buried face down – edge leading."

Tony Reynolds, London N19

*   *   *

A patient goes to the doctor, who diagnoses with the aid of a computer.

After a long wait, the system comes up with:
'There's a lot of it about.'

Valerie Grosvenor Myer, Ely

*   *   *

Q: What do you get when you cross a cow with a computer?

A: A Milk Monitor!

Stephanie Jenkins, Oxford

*   *   *

True Story ...?

On one side of a busy road, a mainframe; on the other, a user in his office.

"Why," he asked, "are response times so long before 9.30am and after 4pm?"

"It's the heavy rush-hour traffic," said the member of the support staff, "it squashes the cables under the road so the signals can't get through."

"I thought that was it," said the user, "but I thought I would ask to make sure."

Robert Clark, Wandsworth, London

*   *   *

The IBM Generation

As IBM is the largest, and almost the oldest, US computer company, you would expect there to be lots of IBM jokes. You would be right. In fact, this section should really be called 'Let's get IBM out of the way early'.

*   *   *

The little boy asked his rich and indulgent father for a cowboy outfit for his birthday, so dad went out and bought him IBM.

*   *   *

In your innocence you probably thought that IBM stood for International Business Machines. In the industry and in IBM they have different and better ideas. Variously ...

    I've Been Moved
    I Buy Money
    I've Been Mugged

... and, of course:

    It's Better Manually.

*   *   *

In 1964, IBM brought out the 360 Series, so named as to indicate it covered all possible angles. In the early seventies it then brought out the 370 Series which IBM wits then said covered all angles plus ten degrees.

*　　　　*　　　　*

At the heart of computers are to be found the instruction repertoires which make them work, otherwise known as the operating systems. Among them once was IBM's MVS, and its various tempting versions:

MVS:	Mine's Very Slow
	or
	Mine's Virtually Stopped
MVS 1:	Mine's a Very Slow One
MVS 1.2:	Mine's a Very Slow One Too

...and you know about the Personal Computer version:

VS.PC:	Vacant Space Permanently Confused

*　　　　*　　　　*

The Archbishop in full regalia found himself at long last at the Gates of Heaven. He was standing just behind a well-dressed, but definitely civilian, civilian.

The Gates opened. St. Peter came out and ushered the civilian in. Before the Gates closed, the Archbishop saw choirs of angels, cherubim and seraphim, and trumpeters in their massed ranks. In the distance God, surrounded by a heavenly light, was gesturing to the civilian to approach and sit at his right hand.

The Gates closed.

Time passed, and the Gates opened again. St. Peter now ushered the Archbishop into Heaven. But where were the massed choirs of angels, the cherubim and seraphim, and the trumpets? It seemed that God, and everybody else, had taken the rest of the day off.

"When I looked before," said the Archbishop in puzzlement, "you remember – the previous entrant – you had massed choirs for him, and God was waiting ..."

"Ah, but *he* was from IBM," said St. Peter.

"But *I* was an Archbishop," said the former Archbishop a little plaintively, "don't I deserve as good a reception?"

"Not really," said St. Peter, "you have to realise that we have a lot of you up here – but that was our first IBM salesman."

*   *   *

She was young, she was beautiful, she was married – and she was with her lawyers seeking a divorce.

"What are the grounds?" said the lawyer.

"Well, after a year of marriage, I'm still a virgin," she replied.

Looking at her, the lawyer found that hard to conceive.*

"What are the circumstances?" he asked.

"Well," she said, "I am married to an IBM salesman. He is a good provider, works hard, works late."

This did not seem a promising start and the lawyer indicated accordingly.

"But," she continued, "every evening when he comes home he sits at the end of the bed and tells me how good it is going to be – and then he falls asleep."

*   *   *

If IBM large-systems salesmen are unlikely to tell the story above, they have been known to tell the following one, which has indeed been around almost for ever:

The DP manager died, went to heaven, and had to admit his profession. Immediately St. Peter sent him straight down to Hell.

"Welcome," said the duty Devil. "You have a

---

* The first time I submitted this to a journal the editor noted this was probably the worst pun she had ever read.

choice of three Hells: an IBM Hell, a Univac* Hell, and an ICL Hell."

"What's the difference?" asked the cautious DP manager.

"Well," said the duty Devil, "the IBM Hell is 22 hours a day of trying to compile a JCL pack for a 1401 program still running a quarter of a century on under emulation on a 3990, followed by two hours of being nailed to a cross and pelted with coal by IBM salesmen.

"The Univac Hell is 22 hours a day of trying to understand communications protocols based on a thinly disguised 1960s Exec 8 manual, followed by two hours of being nailed to a cross and pelted with coal by Univac salesmen.

"The ICL Hell is 22 hours a day of trying to convert a George 3 program to run under ICL's current OS, whatever that is, followed by two hours of being nailed to a cross and pelted with coal by ICL salesmen."

On hearing all this, the DP manager looked worried. A passing Imp, in life a DP operator, took pity and suggested he pick the ICL Hell.

"Why?" asked the DP manager.

"Well," said the Imp, "they never learn. By the time the ICL salesmen have collected the wood to make the cross, found their support engineers and got them to nail the bits together, and then sent to St. Paul for coal, the two hours are almost always over."

*   *   *

* now Unisys

I first found a prolix version of the following in a set of early '50s NATO engineering conference proceedings, in the days when anything and everything that was said by computer people went into the transcript, in case it should eventually be useful.

The Ultimate Computer stood at the end of the Ultimate Computer Manufacturer's production line.

At which point the guided tour eventually arrived.

The Salesman stepped forward to give his prepared patter.

"This," he said, "is the Ultimate Computer. It will give an intelligent answer to any question you may care to ask it."

At which Clever Dick stepped forward – there always is one – and spoke into the Ultimate Computer's microphone.

"Where is my father?" he asked.

There was the whirring of wheels and flashing of lights that the manufacturers always used to impress lay people, and then a little card popped out.

On it were printed the words 'Fishing off Florida.'

Clever Dick laughed.

"Actually," he said, "my father is dead."

It had been a trick question.

The salesman, carefully chosen for his ability to think fast on his feet, immediately replied that he was sorry the answer was unsatisfactory, but as

computers were precise, perhaps he might care to rephrase his question and try again?

Clever Dick thought, went up to the UC and this time said:

"Where is my mother's husband?"

Again there was a whirring of wheels and a flashing of lights.

And again a little card popped out.

Printed on it this time were the words:

'Dead. But your father is still fishing off Florida.'

*　　　　*　　　　*

The IBM salesman and IBM systems analyst went to spend a weekend in the forest, hunting bear.

They hired a log cabin, and when they got there, took their backpacks off and put them inside.

At which point the salesman said to the systems analyst:

"You unpack while I go and find us a bear."

The analyst finished unpacking and then went and sat outside to await events. He did not have to wait for long.

Soon he could hear noises in the forest. The noises got nearer – and suddenly there was the salesman, running across the clearing towards the cabin, pursued by the largest and most ferocious Brown Bear the analyst had ever seen.

"Open the door!" shouted the salesman.

The analyst opened the door.

The salesman ran to the open door, suddenly stopped, and stepped aside.

The Bear, carried by its momentum, continued through the door and disappeared inside.

The salesman promptly shut the door on it, turned, looked at the analyst, and said:

"OK, you skin that one while I go and rustle us up another."

*   *   *

And a final word from IBM themselves (if, of course, you believe *that* ...)

NEW IBM OPERATING SYSTEM

Because so many users have asked for an operating system of even greater capability than VM, IBM announces the Virtual Universe Operating System – OS/VU.

Running under OS/VU, the individual user appears to have not merely a machine of his own, but an entire universe of his own, in which he can set up and take down his own programs, data sets, systems networks, personnel and planetary systems. He need only specify the universe he desires, and the OS/VU system generation program (IEHGOD) does the rest. This program will reside in SYS1.GODLIB. The minimum time for this function is 6 days of activity and 1 day of review. In conjunction with OS/VU, all system utilities have been replaced by one program (IEHPROPHET) which will reside in SYS1.MESSIAH. This program has no listings, it simply knows what you want to do when it is executed.

Naturally, the user must have attained a certain degree of sophistication in the data processing field if an efficient utilization of OS/VU is to be achieved. Frequent calls to non-resident galaxies, for instance, can lead to unexpected delays in the execution of a job. Although IBM, through its wholly owned subsidiary, the United States, is working on a program to upgrade the speed of light and thus reduce the overhead of extra-terrestrial and metadimensional paging, users must be careful for the present to stay within the laws of physics. IBM must charge an additional fee for violations.

OS/VU will run on any xOxx equipped with Extended WARP Feature. Rental is twenty million dollars per cpu-nanosecond.

Users should be aware that IBM plans to migrate all existing systems and hardware to OS/VU as soon as our engineers effect one output that is (conceptually) error-free. This will give us a base to develop an even more powerful operating system, target date 2001, designated "Virtual Reality". OS/VR is planned to enable the user to migrate to totally unreal universes. To aid the user in identifying the difference between "Virtual Reality" and "Real Reality", a file containing a linear arrangement of multisensory total records of successive moments of now will be established. Its name will be SYS1.est.

For more information contact your IBM data processing representative.

Zévar's cartoon strip has been running weekly in France's *01 Informatique* seemingly for ever, and for consistency is the envy of computer publications everywhere. Much of his humour arises from peculiarly French national characteristics and proclivities – and is truly untranslatable. But what follows is indeed easy to puzzle out and is worth doing so – *sans traduction littéraire*.

Zévar: un train nommé désir

Zévar prend son vol

01 Informatique

The Definitive Laws of Computing

(or why computing works ... or does not).

Whoever Murphy was, there is general agreement that his basic Law 'If anything can go wrong, it will' is a masterly observation of fundamental importance about the reality of the world.

Now computing is about laws, precise statements, ordered steps and processes. From the earliest days, therefore, explorations, codifications, and variants of Murphy's Law were to be discovered by those involved with computing.

There are hundreds of them; but first the basic corollaries to Murphy's Law may be stated thus:

1) Everything will go wrong at the same time.
2) If there is any possibility at any time of any one of several things going wrong, then the one that will go wrong will be that one likely to cause the most damage.
3) Left to themselves things will generally go from bad to worse.*
4) Nature always sides with the hidden flaw.
5) If everything seems to be going well, you have obviously overlooked something.

*   *   *

---

* This is no more than a rewrite of the Entropy Law known to every Saturday morning science fiction television watcher as 'The Heat Death of the Universe'.

The corollaries and the computing-related derivatives were discovered by many. In no particular order of importance, just alphabetically, they include: Bouggere, Brooks, Caan, Finagle, Gilb, Granholm, Hoare, Jones, Malik, Meskinen, Osborn, O'Toole, Peter, Sattinger, Shaw ...

But first, Ginsberg's Theorems:

1. You can't win.
2. You can't break even.
3. You can't even quit the game.

Next the general corollaries:

1. (Sattinger): It works better if you plug it in.
2. (Malik)   : If it still does not work, try switching it on.
3. (Caan)   : If all else has failed, why not read the instructions?

And now we can properly begin.

The systems corollary to Murphy's Law:

If anything can go wrong with a system, it will do so generally at the moment that the system becomes indispensable.

The computing variant of the Peter Principle:

Like the human employee, the computer is also subject to the principle. If it does good work at first, there is a strong tendency to promote it to more responsible tasks until it reaches its level of incompetence.

The General System Laws.

The probability of anything happening is in inverse ratio to its desirability. (The Malik observation: This law is itself unreliable)

The amount of expertise varies in inverse proportion to the number of statements understood by the general public.

Meskinen's Law: There's never time to do it right, but always time to do it again.

It is impossible to make things foolproof because fools are so ingenious.

Granholm's definition of *kludge:*

An ill-assorted collection of poorly-matching parts forming a distressing whole.

The Consultant Definition:

A consultant is someone who knows less about your system than you, but gets paid more for telling you how to devise and run it than you could possibly make yourself, even if you devised and ran it properly instead of the way the consultant explained it.

The consultant is sometimes likely to employ some high-powered scientific techniques which he will probably not describe to you. Among them:

Finagle's Constant: This is a multiplier of zero order term which can loosely be described as changing the universe to fit the equation.

The Bouggere* Factor: Here one changes the equation to fit the universe. More classically known as the Smoothing Factor, it has the effect of reducing the subject at issue to nil importance.

The consultant may also well employ Shaw's Principle:

Build a system that even a fool can use and only a fool will want to use it.

*   *   *

And now some general observations ...

Anonymous:

All software, hardware, and systems with the same series number or name must be developed so as to be reliably reproducible. They must always fail in the same way.

The Harvard Law states:

Under the most rigorously controlled conditions of pressure, temperature, humidity, volume, and other variables, the organism will continue to do as it damn well pleases.

Thus Malik's computing derivative of the Harvard Law runs:

Under the most ridiculously controlled conditions of operation, availability of correct and validated data, ability of the operators to cleanly

---

* This name is pronounced as you would expect

hit the right keys in correct order, working hardware, specific routines-in-use bug-cleared software, watchable VDU's and appropriate ribbons and paper in working printer, the system will continue to deliver results as indicated by the first SNAFU* equation; an analysis of the generated answers will always find the system to be basing its calculations on $n + 1$ unknowns.

It will in other words be doing as it damn well pleases.

*   *   *

Weinberg's Law:

If builders built buildings the way programmers write programs, then the first woodpecker that came along would destroy civilisation.

Brooks Law:

Adding manpower to a late software project makes it later.

Hoare's Law:

Inside every large computer program there is a small program struggling to get out.
(The Malik observation of the [private] IBM corollary: Not if we have anything to do with it.)

*   *   *

* SNAFU: Situation Normal, All Fouled Up

The Laws of Commercial Programming:

1) Any given program when running is obsolete.
2) Any given program costs more and takes longer.
3) If a program is useful, it will have to be changed.
4) Any given program will expand to fill all available memory.
5) If a program is useless, it will have to be documented.
6) The value of a program is directly proportional to the weight of its output.*
7) Program complexity will usually grow until it exceeds the capability of the programmers who have to maintain it.
8) Make it possible for programmers to write programs in intelligible English, or any other natural people language, and it will be found that programmers cannot write intelligible English, or any other natural people language.

*   *   *

* The Sixth Law's observation is flawed. On balance, the reverse is true and the Law should read: 'The value of a program is inversely proportional to the weight of its output.'

Norwegian software consultant, academic and author Tom Gilb long ago coined his Laws of Unreliability:

1) Computers are unreliable, but humans are even more unreliable.
   Corollary: At the source of every error blamed on the computer, you will find at least two errors including the error of blaming it on the computer.

2) Any system which depends on human reliability is unreliable.

3) Investment in reliability will increase until it exceeds the probable cost of errors, or until someone insists on getting some useful work done.

*　　　*　　　*

The Ninety/Ninety Rule of Project Schedules:

The first ninety per cent of the task takes ninety per cent of the time, and the last ten per cent takes the other ninety per cent.

Hayne's Law:

Unless the specification states otherwise, we must assume that circuit delay varies in accord with changes in supply voltage, ambient temperature, time, and the Dow-Jones Index.

*　　　*　　　*

The Law of Software Standardisation:

Any software which has been internationally standardised will now only have *n* versions.
The Malik corollary: This also applies to X25, X400, and the ISO seven-layer model.

The Law of Automatic Program Generation:

A program generator will generate any program except the one that you are currently trying to specify.

The Correctness of Bits Law:

In any code or collection of data, the elements that are obviously correct beyond all need of checking will contain the error.
Corollary: In any coded program the modules which are undeniably and indisputably correct are causing the execution errors. (This corollary was made by a student of Ginsberg's).

*   *   *

SNAFU* Equations

1) Given any problem containing n equations, there will always be $n + 1$ unknowns.
2) An object or bit of information most needed will be least available.
3) Any device requiring service or adjustment will be least accessible.
4) Interchangeable devices aren't/won't.
5) In any human endeavour, once you have exhausted all possibilities and fail, there will be one solution, simple and obvious, highly visible to everyone else.
6) Badness comes in waves.

*   *   *

* SNAFU: Situation Normal, All Fouled Up.

Murphy's Hardware Laws:

1) The maintenance engineer will never have seen a model quite like yours before.
2) It is axiomatic that any spares required will have just been discontinued and will be no longer in stock.
3) Any VDU, from the cheapest to the most expensive, will protect a ten pence fuse by blowing first.
4) Any manufacturer making his warranties dependent upon the device being earthed will only supply power cabling with two wires.
5) If a circuit requires n components, then there will be only $n-1$ components in locally-held stocks.
6) A failure in a device will never appear until it has passed final inspection.

*   *   *

Some General Observations on Data Access (or Manual! Manual! Who's Got the Manual?)

Suppose that any important instruction or operations manual is urgently required, it will either have been discarded by whoever was supposedly keeping it safe, or whoever was responsible for it the last time it was sought will now have left the organisation.

The departed will not have told anyone where he put it, even if he knew.

Therefore,

One: As his files are bound to have been raided by those left behind, it follows that the manual sought will now be in the hands of whoever in the organisation is least likely to need it.

Start there.

Two: Suppose the manual is really (and I do mean *really*) urgently required – and is actually found. On opening it you will find that all units of measurement will be in the least usable dimensions; i.e. disc access rates will be given in furlongs per fortnight.

*   *   *

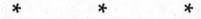

Jones's Law:

The man who can smile when things go wrong, has thought of someone he can blame it on.

Finally ...

Murphy's Funding Law:

Whoever controls the funds makes the rules.

Finally, finally ...

O'Toole's Commentary on Murphy's Law:

Murphy was an optimist.

*   *   *

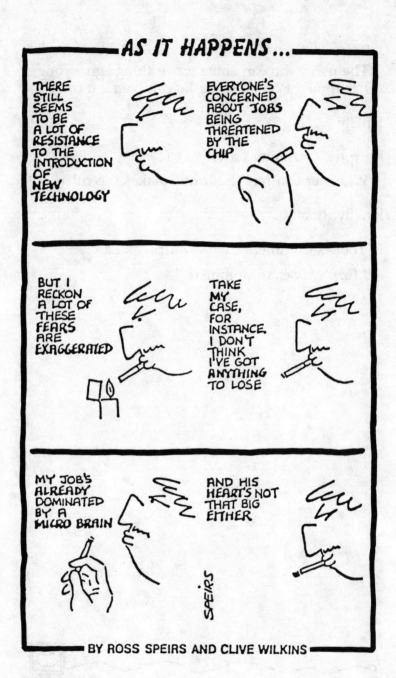

Computing

Management and the Computer

The political management history of a typical large organisation's computing project ...

Stage one:
: Formal conference followed by lunch and copious liquor

Stage two:
: Uncritical acceptance by senior management of everything

Stage three:
: Wild enthusiasm – and unlimited expenses, which are promptly utilised by those on the periphery

Stage four:
: Seeds of senior managerial doubt

Stage five:
: Management disillusion becomes apparent even to the participants

Stage six:
: Total confusion

Stage seven:
: Search for scapegoats

Stage eight:
: At long last ... a presentation of specification

Stage nine:
: Punishment of the innocent

Stage ten:
  Agreement of new terms of reference – the same as the old ones but now written down

Stage eleven:
  Promotion of the non-participants

Stage twelve:
  Maintenance (of whatever little was achieved) by the conscientious

Stage thirteen:
  Proposal for radical restructuring made by the newly-promoted

*   *   *

Remember 'How many Mexicans, Californians, or White Anglo-Saxon Protestants does it take to change a light bulb?' Well, in 1981, the American journal *Infoworld* posed its readers the question: 'How many programmers does it take to change a light bulb?' It was deluged with answers, among them the following:

None: that's a hardware problem.

Two at least: one always changes jobs in the middle of a project.

Three: a programmer to blame it on the hardware and call a customer engineer.
  a customer engineer to blame it on the operating system and call a systems programmer.

a systems programmer to say it is an application problem and the first programmer should re-program the light switch.

Four: one to analyse the problem, one to write the instructions, one to check and debug the instructions, and one to perform the operation.

Twelve: one to change the bulb, one for back up, and ten to write the documentation.

Lastly ...

No programmer would, or could, ever change a light bulb because:

a) it is not part of the job description
b) the light bulb has no addressable memory anyway.

There is, of course, now an IBM PC version:

'How many IBM PC hardware engineers does it take to screw in a light bulb?'

One Hundred: Ten to do it, and ninety to write document number GC57003901 Multitasking Incandescent Source System Facility, of which ten per cent of the pages state 'This page intentionally left blank', and in which twenty per cent of the definitions are in the form: "A whoopdedoo consists of a sequence of non-blank characters separated by blanks."

*   *   *

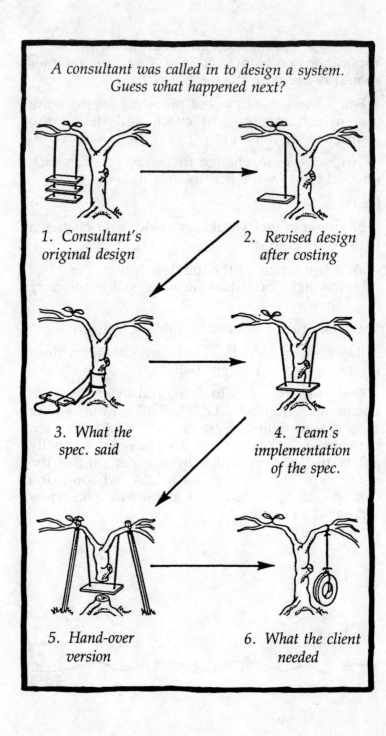

A consultant was called in to design a system.
Guess what happened next?

1. Consultant's
original design

2. Revised design
after costing

3. What the
spec. said

4. Team's
implementation
of the spec.

5. Hand-over
version

6. What the client
needed

The Data-Processing-Information-Services Director/Manager's Guide to Personal Survival.

Go placidly amid the politics and decision-making, and remember what peace there may be in the silence of your own office.

(Remember, too, that if all else fails, there is always an educational course going on somewhere, set in salubrious surroundings – a course you may justifiably attend and for which the organisation will pay.)

As far as possible, do not believe in miracles, but learn to rely on them. Speak convincingly when in doubt, and when in trouble, delegate.

Listen to others, for the dull and ignorant, sometimes even your own staff, can have inside information.

Keep interested in your own career, and take notes of other people's mistakes, however mighty or humble, for they can be a real possession in the changing fortunes of time.

Exercise caution in your affairs, for the organisation is full of trickery. Remember that there is virtue in only giving verbal orders, never committing to storage accessible by others any writings that could ever conceivably be held against you.

(Confine your writing to manuals, ensuring that they should only be comprehensible to you and your staff, and even then not totally comprehensible to them.)

Be yourself. Do not be cynical about profits, for in the face of all trends and economic indicators, governments, revenue authorities, financial controllers, accountants and auditors, you know that with careful programming, they can be as perennial as grass.

Nurture the strength of spirit to shield yourself from divisional cut-backs, but do not distress yourself with imaginings. Even if you are, as you know, only moderately able, you should have allowed for them in your carefully inflated forecasts. What else are spread sheets for?

Take kindly the counsel of the years, gracefully surrendering your naïvety.

Many fears are born of overwork and exclusion from seemingly important meetings. Should this be troublesome to you, you can always join the local computing society and become its President: after all everybody else has. This will impress those set in authority over you, and will ensure that you never have to go through the personal agony of ever having to take a solitary decision solitarily again.

Beyond a wholesome salary indexed to at least the rate of inflation and guaranteed in your contract, an also inflation-proofed pension, and control of a reasonable expense account – where you define what is reasonable – be gentle with yourself.

You are a child of the organisation, no less than the directors, your fellow executives, the union

representatives and your staff.

You have a right to be here, and whether or not it is clear to you, no doubt the structure is unfolding as it should.

Therefore be at peace with your superiors – whoever you conceive them to be, and whatever your actual (as distinct from theoretical) labours and aspirations. In the noisy confusion of the organisation's life, keep peace also with your co-workers and those set under you.

Do not forget that with all its sham, drudgery, and broken dreams, the organisation can still be a never-ending source of increasing real income.

Be seen with enough of the right fellow senior executives in enough of the right meetings and important places: this indicates you are pulling your weight.

Strive to look modest but important, for however old the rule may be, it still has the mark about it of truth enshrined: an ounce of image is worth a pound of performance.

* * *

"Marjorie! It's a personal call by 'Reader's Digest'."

Overheard in Bars ...

The salesman, demonstrating the system to one of the rich and idle, reassures him:

"Don't worry. It's user friendly, but not over familiar."

*   *   *

Then there's that other salesman, demonstrating the system advertised as suitable for the senior managerial desk, who usefully points out that it comes with software capable of playing office politics.

*   *   *

The cleaning lady has what looks like a chip in her hand, and one of the two men crawling around the floor obviously searching for something is looking at it and saying:

"Surely that's not our supercomputer. Where did you find that one?"

*   *   *

You didn't think we could compile a collection of computer jokes without having an Irishman somewhere, did you?

The Englishman, Scotsman and Irishman were having their usual late-night bar session and arguing, futilely as ever. This time the bone of contention was: 'What is man's finest creation?' It was put up, or shut up, time.

Englishman: "No question. It is the Egyptian pyramids. When you remember they were created all those thousands of years ago using only the most primitive of tools, yet they are still standing today."

Scotsman: "It has to be the computer. Computers got man to the Moon, allowed him to pick up a bucket of dust and return to Earth again. Without computers it would not have been possible."

Irishman: "De Termos flask."

Englishman and Scotsman in unison: "The Thermos flask?"

Irishman: "De Termos flask. In the winter, you put in the hot soup and it stays hot. In the summer you put in the cold drink and it stays cold.

"How the bloody hell does it know?"

"Our computer shows no record of you. We hereby declare you a non-person."

You Can Quote Me ...

J.H.: If this is time sharing, give me my share right now.
D.R.: Its not time yet.

Any clod can have the facts, but having opinions is an art.
Charles McCabe

In spite of the recent progress in science, the depths of human imbecility have not yet been plumbed.
H. Ellis

If your boss calls tomorrow, do you want me to find out his name?
L. Briski

Subtlety is the art of saying what you think and getting out of the way before it is understood.
Anonymous

I have finally learned what "upward compatible" means. It means we get to keep all our old mistakes.
Dennie Van Tassel

The VAX 11/785 is bug for bug compatible with the VAX 11/780.
Anonymous

On a Clear Disk you can seek forever.
Jeff Mischinsky

You can't inhibit an open wire.
E. Schmidt

Counting in Octal is just like counting in Decimal
if you don't have any thumbs.
Tom Lehrer

APL is a write-only language. I can write programs
in APL but I can't read any of them.
Roy Keir

You can now buy more gates with less pages of
specification than at any other time in history.
Kenneth Parker

Don't sweat it, it's only ones and zeroes.
P. Skelly

The Second Law of Thermodynamics: If you think
things are in a mess now, just wait.
Jim Warner

The purpose of computing is insight, not numbers.
Richard W. Hamming
The purpose of computing numbers is not yet in
sight.
George E. Forsyth

*   *   *

Electronic Graffiti

Collected over years of browsing through 'bulletin boards' (publicly available databases).

Thought for the Day: As far as we know, our computer has never had an undetected error.
Conrad H. Weisert, Union Carbide Corporation.

Thought for the Winter: Now that the days are shorter, it gets late so much earlier.
Anonymous

When God endowed human beings with brains, he did not guarantee them.

A truly wise man never plays leap-frog with a unicorn.

Beauty is only skin deep, but ugly goes right to the bone.

Now and then an innocent man is sent to the legislature.

If you want to leave your footprints in the sands of time, wear workboots.

An idea is not responsible for the people who believe in it.

Be interested in the future – you will spend the rest of your life there.

And my favourite ...

Might as well be frank, Monsieur. It would take a miracle to get you out of Casablanca.

*   *   *

Two Russian Stories

In the early days of the Russian-Chinese dispute, the men in the Kremlin wished to have some idea of the future of their relations with China.

'What sort of problems will we face with China in the year 2000?' was fed into the very latest Russian supercomputer and its forecasting software.

The computer, after a short hesitation, replied:

'We face no problems of any real importance. All is quiet on the Chinese-Finnish front.'

*　　　*　　　*

I first heard the following in 1968 from a leading Soviet computer representative. I cannot help it being sexist: those were very different days.

After many years of research and development, the Moscow Cybernetics Research Institute came up with the ultimate weighing-machine. It was intelligent: it not only spoke your weight, it did so in your own language – even if you had not spoken! And it also gave dieting instructions.

The obvious place in which to carry out operational trials was Moscow International Airport. It was installed just outside the Arrivals Hall, and the scientists mounted the stairs to the gallery above to observe its performance.

The area they overlooked was spacious and floored with marble. Find such an area in the Soviet Union and there you will find a *Babushka*, a usually much overweight oldish lady perpetually cleaning. This area was no exception.

A plane landed, and eventually the first passenger came out. She was Italian and plump. Spotting the machine she went to stand on its platform.

There was a two second pause before the machine spoke (in Italian):

"Your weight is 72 kilos. You are three or so kilos above what you should be for your size and frame. I suggest you knock off the pasta."

Next came an elegant Frenchwoman. Again there was a two second pause, and then the machine spoke in a flawless Parisian accent:

"Your weight is exactly what it should be for your size and frame. Whatever it is you are doing, continue."

The *Babushka* had been quietly observing all this. After the traffic died down, she took a look around the hall to make sure she was not observed and then went and stood on the platform herself.

The two-second pause stretched out to five and then a plaintive voice said in Russian:

"Would one of you please get off?"

*   *   *

"I suppose one day I'll get round to replacing the whole thing by a silicon chip."

For the Spiritually Minded

A Biblical Dictionary of Computing Terms

Project Proposal:
Your old men shall dream dreams, your young men shall see visions
Joel 2:28

Feasability Study:
Yet what shall I choose I wot not, for I am in a strait betwixt two
Philippians 1:22,23

System Specification:
For which of you ... sitteth not down first and counteth the cost, whether he have sufficient to finish it?
St Luke 14:28

System Audit:
Surely thou hast greatly deceived this thy people?
Jeremiah 4:10

System Design:
And the rain descended, and the floods came, and the winds blew, and beat upon that house: and it fell not: for it was founded on a rock
St Matthew 7:25

Implementation:
And there shall be a time of trouble, such as never was
Daniel 12:1

Program Bugs:
When I would do good, evil is present with me
Romans 7:21

Data Validation:
And there shall in no wise enter into it any thing
that defileth
Revelation 21:27

Error Correction:
Fret not thyself because of evildoers
Psalms 37:1

Resource Allocator:
For I am a man under authority ... and I say to
this man, Go, and he goeth; and to another,
Come, and he cometh; and to my servant, Do
this, and he doeth it
St Matthew 8:9

Seekers after Promotion:
They said unto him, Grant unto us that we may
sit, one on thy right hand, and the other on thy
left hand, in thy glory
St Mark 10:37

Seekers after a Bonus:
Then I looked on all the works that my hands had
wrought, and on the labour that I had laboured to
do and, behold ... there was no profit under the
sun
Ecclesiastes 2:11

*　　　*　　　*

Extracts from the 1010 Commandments of Computing

0010 Thou shalt not make unto thee any *Analog* of any thing that is in the heavens above, or that is in the earth beneath, or that is in the water below: for I, the Lord thy *Computer*, am a *Digital Computer*, visiting the sins of the programmers upon the third, fourth and even the fifth generation machines of them that hate me.

0011 Thou shalt not take the name of the Lord thy *Computer* in vain; for, unto him that taketh the name of the *Computer* in vain, the *Computer* shall send phone bills of £9999994:57 and bank statements of £9999873:21 wherewith to pay them. The *Computer*, in his infinite wisdom, may also do this to perfectly innocent people: for his actions pass all human understanding.

0110 Thou shalt not branch into the midst of a loop, neither shalt thou abolish GO TOs, for the Lord thy *Computer's* appetite is voracious and needs to be satisfied.

0111 Thou shalt not commit adultery with thy computer manager, his wife, his daughters, his sons, or anything that is his, for that way thou risketh withdrawal of thy computer facilities.

1000 Thou shalt not steal thy neighbour's programs, except thou give him a perfunctory acknowledgement in thy thesis or book if he should notice thy theft.

1001 Thou shalt not bear false witness, except on behalf of thy *Computer*. Thou shalt never admit to any outsider that thy *Computer* could possibly make a mistake.

1010 Thou shalt not tamper with control programs without leaving traces, nor overwrite the monitor. Thou shalt not overwrite thy neighbour's files, nor his stored programs, nor his data, nor anything that is his. And more than this, thou shalt not steal, hide, lose or scratch his floppies, borrow his cassette tapes to record 'The Top Twenty', or use them to copy video game programs for friends or profit.

*   *   *

The Software Team-Leader's Prayer

Dear Lord:

Help me to become the kind of leader my Management would like to have me be. Give me the mysterious something which will enable me at all times to satisfactorily explain policies, rules, regulations and procedures to my team members, even when they have never been explained to me.

Help me to teach and train the uninterested and dimwitted without ever losing my patience or my temper.

Give me that love for my fellow men and women which passeth all understanding, so that I may lead the recalcitrant, obstinate, no-good worker

into the paths of righteousness by my own example and by soft persuading remonstrance, instead of kicking them up the fundament.

Instil into my inner being tranquillity and peace of mind, that no longer will I wake from my restless sleep in the middle of the night crying out "What has the Boss got that I have not – and how did he get it?"

Teach me to smile if it kills me.

Make me a better leader by helping me to develop larger and greater qualities of understanding, tolerance, sympathy, wisdom, perspective, equanimity, mind-reading and second sight.

And when, dear Lord, thou has helped me to achieve the high pinnacle my Management has prescribed for me, and when I have become the paragon of all supervisory virtues in this earthly world, dear Lord, *move over*.

AMEN.

*   *   *

True Stories

There is, of course, the (apocryphal?) anecdote about the American spelling-checker program, SPLT, which has an acknowledgement on the title page of its manual:

'Our thanks to Fred for proof-reading SPLT which checks for spelling misteaks'.

But with computers the truth, as elsewhere, is always stranger than fiction. The following selection just hints at the rich variety of idiocy ...

Prognostication Problems

Alan Turing, the mathematician and theoretical father of computing, was once asked how many computers the UK would eventually have: he thought no more than six. His calculation was based on the premise that there were not otherwise enough mathematicians around to handle and cope with the output from any more than that.

Thomas J. Watson, the founder of IBM, had an even smaller figure: he thought, on the best of advice, that the company was unlikely to make more than five.

Incidentally, while everybody tells jokes about computer salesmen, did you know that Lord Bowden (Ferranti's, and therefore the world's, first computer salesman) is fond of telling the story of the days when the industry's salesforce was so small that it was outnumbered 100 per cent by that of the British lighthouse industry – which employed two salesmen.

*   *   *

Editorial Comment

From *The Wall Street Journal,* June 1974.

A Canadian from Dundas had his pocket picked back in 1970 losing his social insurance card, birth certificate, and driver's licence. The pickpocket, apparently an enterprising sort, used this identification for a series of misdeeds.

As a result the Dundas man wound up with a criminal record in the files of the Royal Canadian Mounted Police and began to receive bills from the Canadian Revenue Department for unpaid taxes on jobs he had never held.

Accordingly, so his Representative told the Canadian Commons recently, he asked the government for a new social insurance number. An official replied that the social insurance computer just couldn't be programmed to do that.

"The only way out," said the official, "was for the man from Dundas to change his name."

The Wall Street Journal's comment on all this was simple:

People who know remind us that computers are really just very elaborate idiots which can only do what they have been told to do. But why is it that when they become enmeshed in the workings of a large organisation, they tend to drag their masters down to their own level?

*　　　*　　　*

Directory Enquiries

In the early '60s, the Queen was asked to make the UK's first-ever official and ceremonial STD telephone call. (It is with STD, of course, that all this telecommunications-tied computing becomes possible.)

The Minister responsible and accompanying her was then called the Postmaster General. His name was Ernest Marples.

The call was to be made from Bristol to Scotland where the Queen was to speak to the Lord Provost of Glasgow.

The Queen was handed a number to dial.

She looked at Ernest Marples and said:

"Postmaster, I do not have much of a head for numbers. What happens if I misdial?"

"Ma'am," said Marples, "on this occasion it doesn't matter what number you dial, you will still get the Lord Provost of Glasgow."

*   *   *

In the early days of on-line communications-oriented computing which followed this event, the computer bureau thought up a new maintenance wrinkle. In the event of a line interruption, the system was programmed to dial and call the maintenance engineer directly on a different line.

This, they told their customers, would ensure 24-hour round-the-clock service.

One Saturday a line went down.

The computer called the service engineer – and got a reply from his telephone answering machine. He had gone fishing.

The computer and telephone answering machine are believed to have conversed unhappily with each other till the Monday morning.

*   *   *

According to *Computagram*, a recent issue of the US long-distance telephone company AT&T's Research Journal contained, in its section Human Factors & Behavioural Science, an article entitled: "Effects of shape and size of knobs on maximal hand-turning forces applied by females."

*   *   *

Entymological Etymology

Rear Admiral Grace Hopper, US Navy (Rtd) (often cited as the world's first professional, paid-for-programming, programmer), began her career on the Naval Ordnance Computer Project at Harvard during World War II.

The machine was officially called the Automatic Sequence Controlled Calculator, or ASCC, and contained bank upon bank of relays to act as switches.

More popularly known as the Harvard Mk1, it was devised and run by a martinet, Howard Aiken. He insisted that every event that occurred to his precious machine was entered into a log.

One hot afternoon, a fault arose. Grace Hopper traced it to a particular bank of relays, where she found a dead – electrocuted – moth caught between the jaws of one relay.

She took the moth out, stuck it solemnly in the log, wrote the time by the side of it and underneath her first claim to immortality.

'De-bugging.'

*　　　　*　　　　*

Incidentally, one of the oldest jokes of all time in this field is of the two female bugs talking over the equivalent of the electronic garden fence. One is looking sad and pensive, the other supportive and helpful.

"Don't worry," says the latter, "I have been in this program for years and they have not caught or found me yet."

*   *   *

Bad Timing

Ever hear of Deuce? It was built by what was then English Electric. Originally it was about eight feet high, five feet wide and eighteen feet long.

It had over 1000 valves. The innards then having to be accessible for servicing, all the engineering was closed off behind cabinet doors. This was necessary also for safety reasons as more than 600 volts went through it.

A party was being shown round the computer room; parties were always being shown round the computer room. The guide, bored as ever, explained to them that the machine was in fact a dummy and that the calculations it performed were really done by a man sitting inside using a calculator (old style).

"Hey Presto." The guide opened the door. Sure enough, there tucked away inside was a man with a calculator.

It is not recorded whether the visitors took computing and computers seriously ever again.

"Sperry Univac? We've just found an exciting new use for it!"

Word Games

From *The Times*

Sir, How rightly did her Majesty in her Christmas broadcast refer to computers that cannot generate compassion! The East Midlands Gas Board has recently addressed a letter to my father, who died nine months ago, thus:

'Dear Mr Hodgkinson decd'.

I am interested to know what kind of reply is expected.
Yours faithfully,
J. C. HODGKINSON

*   *   *

A computer translator become famous for construing 'out of sight, out of mind' as 'invisible idiot', so there should be at least some mention of the business studies student who translated 'environmentalist lobby' as 'surrounding porch'.

*   *   *

In the early days of computer translation, when the machines used to operate by syllable comparison, the main American program used to translate from Russian to English – the one the US Air Force used for Russian manual translation – found the name Ava Gardner in a Russian document and came up with Ava Burning Bottom.

*   *   *

From *The Daily Telegraph*

W. H. Smith's new computer, christened Book-finder, was being shown off at the company's Swindon offices when it was asked to find a book with the word "cat" or "dog" in its title. The machine excelled: "Catholic Dogma", it suggested.

*   *   *

"First you forget logarithms. Then you forget how to do long division. Then the multiplication table begins to go ..."

Datamation

The *Abacus* Time Line

In 1986, the editors of *Abacus,* the New York-based international computer professionals' quarterly, gave their forecasts for the coming decade in computing. It included:

1986 – Abacus Time Line is denounced as frivolous
   – End of Fortran predicted
   – Star Wars programming started
   – South Africa bans black on white computer displays
   – Manufacturer announces the unary computer with half the symbols and twice the speed of binary

1987 – End of Cobol predicted
   – US Department of Defense (DoD) orders ultra-high-speed printer using invisible ink

1988 – End of Fortran predicted
   – Star Wars software certified correct
   – Stanford Professor discovers purpose of Local Area Networking
   – DoD classifies Stanford LAN report as Top Secret

1989 – End of Cobol predicted
   – Last human Grandmaster disqualified for playing too slowly in international chess competition
   – First computer admitted to graduate school and seeks degree in English Literature

1990 – End of Fortran predicted
   – IBM acquires 14 failing firms, including Exxon and General Motors
   – IBM buys Florida
   – Star Wars software tested
1991 – End of Cobol predicted
   – Star Wars software reprogramming started
   – US Justice Department sues IBM for restraint of trade
   – IBM acquires Justice Department
1992 – End of Fortran predicted
   – Star Wars corrected software certified correct
   – Last university mathematics department renamed 'Department of Computer Science'
1993 – End of Cobol predicted
   – CIA indicted for unauthorised entry into 14-year-old's secret computer files
   – Last high school grammar and spelling class replaced by word processing course
1994 – End of Fortran predicted
   – Star Wars corrected software tested
   – Star Wars corrected software reprogramming started
1995 – End of Cobol predicted
   – DoD announces unbreakable secret encryption scheme
   – Charles Babbage, 9-year-old MIT undergraduate breaks new DoD code
   – DoD prohibits publication of Babbage solution

1996 – End of Fortran predicted
– Japan announces 13th Generation
Computer Project
– DoD announces 13th Generation
Computer Project
1997 – End of Cobol predicted
– Ada documentation exceeds capacity of
all toxic waste dumps
– Abacus Time Line proved correct in
every detail

*   *   *

Some Technical Definitions

Advanced Technology: It's too complicated for me

Experience: Obsolescence

Assembly Language: Installation leaflet found inside computer packaging

Delayed: Being rewritten

Extensive choice: You can order either last year's, this year's or next year's

Now Available: (software house usage) We reckon we can finish the software before they can deliver your hardware

Shipped: Moved from the assembly line to the check-out line

Installed: Sitting in crates in the customer's office

Operational: Taken out of crates and (mostly) plugged together

Fact: This is the way they have done it in the past. Not to be confused with 'This is what is stated in the manual'

Programming standards:	Banners flown on poles above manufacturers' premises
Software specification:	Listings (q.v.)
Hardware specification:	Listings (q.v.)
Software support:	Membership card to a club where they exchange lists of bugs
Hardware support:	Membership card to a club where they exchange the bugs themselves
Software fault:	See Hardware fault
Hardware fault:	See Software fault
Listings:	A detailed form of accurate information believed to be available somewhere abroad. Not to be confused with Manuals (q.v.)
Manuals:	A form of information available locally but out of date
CPU:	A random number generator
Modem:	Sophisticated equipment used to simulate the sound of a disconnected telephone

Mistake: An occurrence caused by someone other than you or me, or, alternatively, by you. The effects create problems large and small for both of us, or, alternatively, small problems for one of us and large problems for you. Remedial action has to be taken by someone other than us two, or alternatively, certainly not by me

Programmer: 1) A person who spends his time trying to explain to the computer the imaginative fantasies of the systems analyst. This involves translating from one unintelligible series of hieroglyphics to another
2) The incompetent writing the incomprehensible
3) An installation-owned error generating system

Feature: A surprising property of a program: 'That's not a bug, that's a feature'

Bit decay: This is a disease the existence of which was first deduced when it was observed that un-used programs stop working after a variable length of time

Jargon: What the managers talk when they don't know what is going on

Executive Summary: An erudite and evasive condensation of several abstract, disconnected, and ambiguous thoughts

*　　　*　　　*

Software Engineering: A Fable*

A computer scientist is given the problem:
'BUILD A FORK WITH THREE PRONGS.'
After some formalisation he arrives at the picture
(1) as a semantic model.

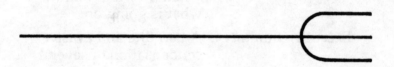

He discovers there is also a fork with *four prongs*
(2) in use, and immediately sees the generalisation
to *n prongs*.

(2)

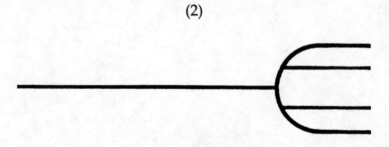

Objections that *n* is variable are met by saying
that '*n* is determined at run time'. So he invents
an instrument that is potentially a rake.

* With acknowledgement to Prof. F. L. Bauer and *Honeywell's Journal*.

(3) The Rake's Progress

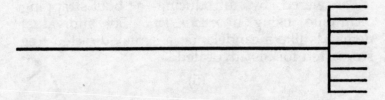

But instead of wasting time to apply it, he leaps forward to a *recursive fork*, after he has realised that, in principle, a *2-pronged fork* is enough.

(4)

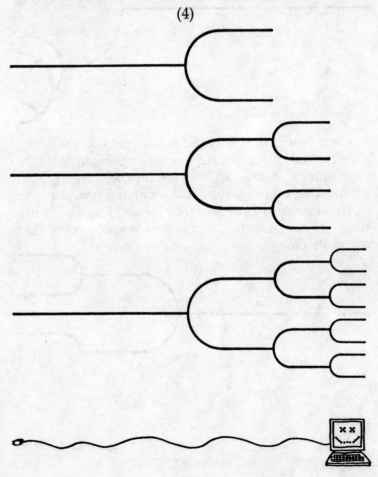

The question of how to manufacture such a fork is answered by introducing a boot-strapping technique using a *macro fork*. For individual demands like a candelabra, a syntax-directed tree structured fork is advocated.

(5)

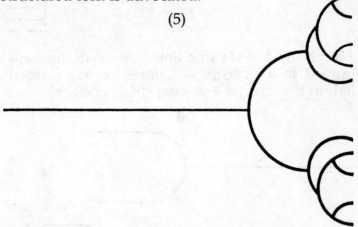

Then the computer scientist gets completely sidetracked by working on the problem of self-reproducing forks. In the meantime there is still an unsatisfied demand for the initial *3-pronged fork*.

This demand is finally met by accident, with the help of a *recursive 4-pronged fork that has lost one of its prongs*.

(6)

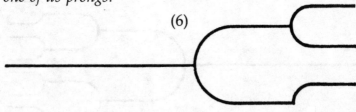

For Experts Only

The Programmer's Revenge

It was the early days of terminals and computer time sharing and the system kept going down, seemingly for no particular reason.

It was happening too frequently for comfort and mischief was suspected.

Mischief was verified.

Mischief was a program called RH BOMB, one always in the system when it went down, printing out 'TSS' (standing for Time Sharing System) 'has gone down.'

A resident programmer with initials RH was seriously spoken to, and the trouble ceased.

Some months later, another programmer browsing through program listings came upon another called RH BOMB.

Not wishing to get RH unnecessarily into trouble he called it up and typed LIST RH BOMB.

The terminal reacted immediately. No listing. Instead, on the VDU appeared ...

'TSS has gone down'.

Then the terminal went dead. Whatever he typed, there was no response.

This was incredible. A program so virulent that even a simple call to list contents wiped out the system.

Panic.

The panic was premature.

The new RH BOMB was a simple program.

TSS had only gone down at the one terminal.

On being queried, all RH BOMB did was to instruct the CPU to send a continuous set of clock pulses to the terminal seeking to list RH BOMB. This effectively locked it, so it could never signal back its readiness for its next task.

What happened to RH this time around is not recorded.

*   *   *

And a Final Word for Computing's Masochists – the UNIX Supporters Club

NAME
flog – speed up a process

SYNOPSIS
flog [–ln] [–am] [–u] process-id ...

DESCRIPTION
Flog is used to stimulate an improvement in the performance of a process that is already in execution.

The *process-id* is the process number of the process that is to be disciplined.

The value *n* of the l keyletter argument is the flagellation constant, i.e., the number of *lashes* to be administered per minute. If this argument is omitted, the default is 17, which is the most random random number.

The value *m* of the a keyletter argument is the number of times the inducement to speed up is to be *administered*. If this argument is omitted, the default is one, which is based on the possibility that after *that* the process will rectify its behaviour of its own volition.

The presence of the u keyletter argument indicates that *flog* is to be *unmerciful* in its actions. This nullifies the effects of the other keyletter arguments. It is recommended that this option be used only on extremely stubborn processes, as its over-use may have detrimental effects.

FILES
Flog will read the file */have/mercy* for any entry containing the process-id of the process being speeded-up. The file can contain whatever supplications are deemed necessary, but, of course, these will be totally ignored if the u keyletter argument is supplied.

SEE ALSO
On Improving Process Performance by the Administration of Corrective Stimulation, *CACM*, vol. 4, 1657, pp. 356-654.

DIAGNOSTICS
If a named process does not exist, *flog* replies "flog you" on the standard output. If *flog kill*(II)s the process, which usually happens when the u keyletter argument is supplied, it writes "rip", followed by the process-id of the deceased, on the standard output.

BUGS
Spurious supplications for mercy by the process being flogged sometimes wind up on the standard output, rather than in */shut/up*.

*　　　　*　　　　*

"It insisted on taking full responsibility."

from the collection of John Pascoe

And, Finally ...

... relaxen, und watchen das Blinkenlights.
or
The more things change, the more they stay the same.

It is called The Connection Machine, a still somewhat experimental parallel processor of immense power. It is best described as, indeed looks like, a cube of cubes.

There is one at MIT, Cambridge, Massachusetts. Naturally all those with computing interests go to look at it, a colleague among them.

The lights were flashing, so he stood in the doorway, looked at the operator at his console in the control room next door, and asked:

"What is it working on?"

"It's not," he was told.

"But the lights are flashing," he said.

The operator flicked some switches, then pushed his chair back, came over and looked.

The lights were still flashing.

"Oh," he said, "it's just thinking.

"We hate it when it does that."

*   *   *